THE LOST CHILD

OZARK POEMS

Also by Wesley McNair

POETRY

The Faces of Americans in 1853 (1984)
The Town of No (1989)
My Brother Running (1993)
Talking in the Dark (1997)
Fire (2002)
The Ghosts of You and Me (2006)
Lovers of the Lost: New & Selected Poems (2010)

POETRY — LIMITED EDITIONS

Twelve Journeys in Maine (1992)
The Dissonant Heart (1995)

NONFICTION

Mapping the Heart: Reflections on Place and Poetry (2003)
A Place on Water (with Robert Kimber and
        Bill Roorbach, 2004)
The Words I Chose: A Memoir of Family and Poetry (2012)

The Lost Child

OZARK POEMS

Wesley McNair

DAVID R. GODINE · *PUBLISHER*
BOSTON

Published in 2014 by
David R. Godine, Publisher
Post Office Box 450
Jaffrey, New Hampshire 03452

LIBRARY OF CONGRESS
CATALOGING-IN-PUBLICATION DATA

McNair, Wesley.
[Poems. Selections]
The lost child : Ozark poems / by Wesley McNair.
   p.   cm.
ISBN-13: 978-1-56792-519-7 (alk. paper)
ISBN-10: 1-56792-519-7 (alk. paper)
I. Title. II. Title: Ozark poems.
PS3563.C388A6 2014
811'.54—dc23
2014003170

FIRST EDITION
Printed in the United States

The characters in Part II of this book are invented, except for my mother, whom I call by her real name, Ruth. She came from the Ozarks of southern Missouri, where she had many relatives. These poems are to remember her and the homeplace that shaped her.

ACKNOWLEDGMENTS

Thanks to the following magazines, in which poems of this collection have appeared: *The American Poetry Review*: "The American Flag Cake," "The Four-Point Crown," "Gratitude," "The Lost Child"; *The Café Review*: "Her Secret"; *Poetry*: "When She Wouldn't"; *The Sewanee Review*: "Dancing in Tennessee," "Graceland," "Why I Carried My Mother's Ashes."

Contents

I · When She Wouldn't

WHEN SHE WOULDN'T

When her recorded voice on the phone
said who she was again and again to the piles
of newspapers and magazines and the clothes

in the chairs and the bags of unopened mail
and garbage and piles of unwashed dishes.

When she could no longer walk
through the stench of it, in her don't-need-nobody-
to-help me way of walking, with her head

bent down to her knees as if she were searching
for a dime that had rolled into a crack

on the floor, though it was impossible to see
the floor. When the pain in her foot she disclosed
to no one was so bad she could not stand

at her refrigerator packed with food and sniff
to find what was edible. When she could hardly

even sit as she loved to sit, all night
on the toilet, with the old rinsed diapers
hanging nearby on the curtainless bar

of the shower stall, and the shoes lined up
in the tub, falling asleep and waking up

while she cut out newspaper clippings
and listened to the late-night talk
on her crackling radio about alien landings

and why the government had denied them.
When she drew the soapy rag across the agonizing

ache of her foot trying over and over to wash
the black from her big toe and could not
because it was gangrene.

When at last they came to carry my mother
out of the wilderness of that house

and she lay thin and frail and disoriented
between bouts of tests and x-rays,
and I came to find her in the white bed

of her white room among nurses who brushed
her hair while she looked up at them and smiled

with her yellow upper plate that seemed to hold
her face together, dazed and disbelieving,
as if she were in heaven,

then turned, still smiling, to the door
where her stout, bestroked younger brother

teetered into the room on his cane, all the way
from Missouri with her elderly sister
and her bald-headed baby brother,

whom she despised. When he smiled back
and dipped his bald head down to kiss her,

and her sister and her other brother hugged her
with serious expressions, and her childish
astonishment slowly changed

to suspicion and the old wildness returned
to her eye because she began to see

this was not what she wanted at all,
I sitting down by her good ear holding her hand
to talk to her about going into the home

that was not her home, her baby brother winking,
the others nodding and saying, Listen to Wesley.

When it became clear to her that we were not
her people, the ones she had left behind
in her house, on the radio, in the newspaper

clippings, in the bags of unopened mail,
in her mind, and she turned her face away

so I could see the print of red on her cheek
as if she had been slapped hard.
When the three of them began to implore

their older sister saying, Ruth, Ruth,
and We come out here for your own good,

and That time rolls around for all of us,
getting frustrated and mad because they meant,
but did not know they meant, themselves too.

When the gray sister, the angriest of them,
finally said through her pleated lips

and lower plate, You was always
the stubborn one, we ain't here to poison you,
turn around and say something.

When she wouldn't.

II · The Lost Child

GRACELAND

Once, in the poverty of the Ozarks,
my aunt Mae's baby brother,
her mother's favorite, stole a ten
dollar bill from his father's wallet.
"Tell him you done it," her mother
said to her. "He won't whip you."

But he did. Aunt Mae was nobody's
favorite. When she stepped in
to stop her husband Lyle
from punching one of their sons,
Lyle went right on swinging.
"That's how I got my nose broke,"

Mae says, almost as if it was her fault,
looking inside herself at the past,
the arms of the fan above our heads
in the lamplight, swinging. Slowly
I understand she hated my Uncle Lyle,
the man the neighbors loved, for years;

part of her sits with me among smiling
family portraits in her farmhouse,
comparing this summer's to last
summer's hot weather, while

the other part is down in the cellar
of her mind among old memories

she's kept like preserves in the dark –
here, her mother telling her to lie
when she was twelve, there, Lyle
beating up a son, or trying
to stare her down in the rear view
mirror on the day Mae drove him

and her mother, against their will,
to Graceland. "This ain't the way home
from Wilmer's," Mae says, slow-talking
like Lyle, enjoying how he begins
to figure out where she's taking them.
"I been there before," says her mother,

beside him in the back seat, as upset
as he is, "and it ain't nothin.'" Aunt Mae,
a farm woman who only had all-day
chores and big-bellied Lyle
when she first saw Elvis shake his hips
on TV, must have been determined

not to turn around now, but
in her story, it's all about Jo-Lynn,
her youngest daughter, in the front
of the car with her, almost peeing
her pants to get inside Elvis's mansion.
Which is why Jo-Lynn ends up crying

her poor eyes out at the gate,
Mae says, when they discover Graceland
is closed, nobody there but some

fat guy in a black wig and a white
suit trying to sell them a painting
of the King on velvet. Mae is just

eighty-seven remembering the sad moment
when she held Jo-Lynn in her arms,
shutting her eyes so she couldn't
see Lyle or her smug mother watching
from the car, the end of her story,
though her story and mine goes on

to the little wonder of how she has made
the house cool for me, her weekend
visitor, despite the Missouri heat
by latching both outside doors
and opening the back window, where
there's a chilly spot the fan pulls in

around us, Mae says. "Do you feel it?"
And I tell her I do, both of us silent
in the pleasure of it, one light on
over her chair, and one light over mine.

THE RUN DOWN 17
INTO PHOENIX

Some nights, Jo-Lynn told Floyd before their marriage,
she got so lonely waiting for her first husband,
the salesman, to come home from the road,
she couldn't stop her teeth from chattering. Jo-Lynn
was the sensitive type, which was what Floyd liked
about her, so he swore he would give up trucking

as soon as he could pay off the truck, but for now,
he asked, what did she think of traveling with him
in Road Hog, his semi, just the two of them,
on his long hauls? When he took her into the room
behind the cab to show off its waterbed, computer,
microwave and LCD TV, she was amazed by the space,

and it turned out to be fun riding with Floyd
in the early morning as he hooked up with 44 out
of the Ozarks and headed west, surprising her every so
often by pulling on the horn. Still, she couldn't avoid
the sad, lost feeling she got when she saw nothing
for miles except a vehicle or a sign coming slowly

toward them out of the flat horizon as the road sped
under the truck. Never mind, Floyd was always
right there beside her, and when they hit a swarm

of exits going every which-way outside some city
and she got scared, he would squeeze her hand and say
how good it was to sit by her side up in the sky

above all the cars lamming around below. One day,
to show he was serious about settling down together,
he turned with a full load right into the nice development
Jo-Lynn wanted to go look at in Amarillo, Texas,
making a deposit on the large corner lot she liked
with no further ado. Now when the tires moaned

and the wind shrieked at the windows, she could be
somewhere else, namely, the home she was planning
on a notepad in her lap. Crazy as things got with all
the back and forth between Floyd's trailer in Fowler
and the house in progress in Amarillo, she had found
her calling, no idle dream to escape the motion

of the truck, but 2500 actual square feet, including
a play room she designed for her grandchildren,
and a dog house, as the builder called it, above the door
with its own cape roof, which he threw in for free.
Floyd upped his hours while Jo-Lynn, who was hungry
to furnish the rooms, stayed home, as she had begun

to call it, emailing him about the his-and-hers leather
recliners she'd located online, or the big screen
recreation center she got on sale, and one night,
after Floyd had parked for the night off the thruway
in Albuquerque, he clicked open her excited message
about finding the perfect place for the bear he'd shot

on a hunting trip and given its own room in the trailer.
Imagine it, she said, behind the plant in the entryway.
The next morning, as luck would have it, Floyd spotted
a closed-up Indian museum with life-size plastic bears
outside, which they offered to him just for the diesel
to haul them away, as he put it in his email, using

all capital letters and exclamation points. After that,
there were bears and bear memorabilia all through
the downstairs and out on the lawn. What she liked
especially was how they never moved. The commuters
would leave the driveways around her in the development
each day, and in the early mornings after Floyd returned

for a pit-stop, Road Hog would chug quietly off
past the sidewalks as if it could hardly wait to reach
the freeway, yet there the bears would be, standing
or sitting in the grass exactly where she had put them.
Wouldn't it be great, she emailed Floyd one evening
while gazing at them out the window of the dog house

where she kept her laptop and could view them best,
to have a stream running by, so it would be like they
were part of nature in some ancient time? Come see
how your new Grampy and I spent our vacation,
she wrote to her grandchildren on her Facebook page,
posting photographs of the bears, which now looked

as if they were drinking or washing themselves
in the stream she had made with a kit from Home
Depot; then she posted pictures of the play room
with its big box of toys. But this year, their second
in Texas, Floyd was driving so much there had not
actually been a vacation, and her daughter wrote back

with much love and a smiley-face from Missouri
that with all the driving she and her husband did
during the week to their jobs in Springfield, they
hardly had time to visit the old Grampy and his wife
in Jeff City. It had never occurred to Jo-Lynn
until now that her grandchildren might not come

at all, ever, she wrote to Floyd, starting to cry when
she read the words she had just typed on her lit-up
computer in a darkness that was so deep she couldn't
even see the bears. Wherever you may be tonight,
she added, and cried some more as she pictured him
hurtling down the freeway inside a shaft of headlights

somewhere west of Texas, because after all her effort
to create a place her new husband would come home to,
she'd begun to realize she was always alone, just
like she was with her first husband before. Everybody
is going, going, going, Jo-Lynn wrote in tears,
and all I ever wanted was for the going to stop.

Hard as those words were for Floyd as he read them,
exhausted in the bedroom of the truck at 2 A.M.,
well after his wife's bedtime, the hardest ones
came next, where Jo-Lynn confessed her teeth
had started chattering again, the very thing Floyd
promised during their courtship he would never allow.

You got to be kidding me, no way, he said to himself
about the teeth, wide awake now as he turned off
his safety lights and got behind the wheel to drive west,
all night if he had to, with his load so he could make it
back to Amarillo by late the next day or early the next.
It wasn't easy for Floyd to be traveling in the opposite

direction from Jo-Lynn after the email she wrote.
At first he almost felt his own teeth begin to chatter
as he drove in the dark, but he consoled himself
thinking how happy he could make Jo-Lynn,
whenever he got home, by putting in a waterfall
with a naturalistic pool beneath it for her bears,

and then, booming along by himself with no other
traffic and his foot on the gas, he began to get
his old feeling that Road Hog was turning to air,
and he couldn't avoid a touch of pride checking
his watch to discover the time he was making,
his best ever, on the run down 17 into Phoenix.

THE ABDUCTION

Allowed back into her house at last in December
after her two-month stay at the acute care center,
Ruth has so much to do, she refuses to wait for herself
to wake up in the morning, and dress, and roll
on her walker out to her chair in the living room. Let
the stupid ones waste their whole lives lying in bed,

sleeping. She's going to sit right here by the bags
Chrystal has dragged from the dumpster back into
her house until she's emptied and sorted through every
last one. Never mind she falls asleep now and then,
this is the chair's fault because it won't allow her
to sit up straight, and the fault of social services

for making such a fuss over safety and sanitation
that her things had to be bagged up and thrown out
in the first place, as if what she'd been saving all
these years were nothing but trash. Chrystal, more
like a daughter than her own daughter, knows different,
and so does Robert, Ruth's new boyfriend. They'd

understand why, when Ruth wakes up in the night
sitting in her chair to discover some old, unopened
bills in her hands, she has to wipe away a tear
of anger. How exactly is she supposed to keep records

for her plant and shrub business by tossing bills away?
Then she leans down to a bag of clothes by her walker

to free a perfectly good shirt that has caught her eye,
and later, as the furnace rumbles on, making a cracking
sound in the baseboard radiators, she wakes to find
she's holding a pair of scissors and a jagged, yellow
article she's cut out from a newspaper, recalling now
the headline: "An Expert Questions the Quality

of Nursing Homes." Reading it aloud to herself,
she feels the hot urgency of justice rise in her chest
until it pops her ears – proof right here in print
she was correct all along about those places,
and that her two brothers, her sister, and her son,
who conspired to put her into one of them, just

because of a little circulation problem in her legs,
needed to become experts in minding their own damned
business, which is exactly what she writes on each
copy of the article she makes with her old copier,
rolling back to her chair along the pathway, carrying
stamps and four envelopes. Anyone could see she's back

as good as new by the headway she's made, recovering
whole stacks of mail and newspapers, a mound of socks
and underpants that only need washing, and some half-
empty sacks of lime for the pansies and forsythias
Ruth and Robert are planning to sell at her nursery
in New Hampshire next spring. Nudging her chair

toward a new lot of the cinched-up green bags, Ruth
can't help noticing that they themselves resemble
the buds of great flowers, straining to blossom.

They seem to understand how important it is
for her to begin her new life, now that her troubles
are over, and her eyes moisten with gratitude

as she thinks of all those who are on her side,
supporting her, Chrystal, who has appropriated
the truck, so she can drive it over and take Ruth
shopping every two weeks, just charging her for upkeep
and the gas, and Robert, who has not only offered
to fix up the nursery but to take the place over,

and makes his own beer, just like her husband Paul
used to do, bringing over samples for her to try.
Ruth's younger sister Mae, in her eighties and still
stuck in the Ozarks, wouldn't believe that Robert, half
Ruth's age, kissed her on the cheek on his last visit,
even though he's married, neither of them caring

to mention his wife. Some people, like the snotty
woman from the visiting nurse program that Ruth
fired on the spot two days ago for her warnings
about falling down in the mess she was making, don't
have a clue about this all-day, all-night job of sorting
and how demanding it is, but Robert knows without

Ruth having to tell him, and sometimes knows what
she wants before she does, like when he brought her
the book about flying saucers and the End Times,
so she could follow up on the radio talk show
that explained how Jesus and the original saints
were actually astronauts. "We think just alike,"

she said during a late-night call to her friend Edie,
who is exactly her age and birth sign, and thinks
just like her, too, but tonight, Ruth calls no one.
How could she describe this gratitude that keeps
on growing until she is crying all over again,
or explain the connection she's beginning to feel

with everything she lifts out of a bag or off
the floor – the knot of used dishrags, the lost can
of macaroni among the empty cans, a stiff rubber
boot that matches its mate – as if when she examines
each rescued object, magnified by her tears,
the past suddenly becomes the present,

and time has not happened to her at all – as if
she is alive, beyond grief, in the very way she now
discovers in the old church bulletin for an Advent
service, reading its headline over and over in her
astonishment. "We that remain and are alive,"
it says, "shall be caught up together with the others

in the clouds." This is when Ruth hears the voices
of the others, outside where the bright light is,
and she pops the old screen door open and rolls
out to find them. She is so hot now all over her body
she does not feel the cold, and in the very second
she waves up at them in the long beam of light,

she finds herself inside a large floating disc, looking
straight down through the clouds that swirl around
her window. There is a small, sad girl in the Ozarks
waving upward outside a shack she wants to escape,
but the toy on wheels by her side (Ruth remembers
no toys) gradually turns into a walker, and the girl,

into a sad old woman, waving upward in the hope
of escaping from herself. "Hello up there, hello,"
says an exhausted voice Ruth thinks at first is her own
voice as the disc slowly lifts beyond the clouds
to shoot through the dark, then she shudders
and blinks and turns to the rapturous others.

THE FOUR-POINT CROWN

After the car wreck that killed her mother and older
sister, Allie's dad forgot all about the Junior Hunters
Four-Point Crown contest he had signed her up for,
and so did Allie, feeling a loneliness she didn't dare
think about and watching her dad go somewhere
else in his eyes and stay there for the whole

summer, like it was the end of him, too. Finally
the pastor came and said God could take the stone
off the tomb her father had made for himself,
but he had to push from the inside. "You can't go on,
Leroy Sykes," the pastor said, "with a stone over
your heart." Then her dad, who seldom talked, started

talking to Allie so much about his feelings and how hard
he was going to try to push on the stone, she worried
more than ever. Didn't she think her mother would want
him to get some use out of the one-room day care
center, now just sitting in the backyard? he asked.
He phoned up two guys from work at the milk plant

in Cabool, and they hauled her mom's place
of business for ten years into the woods where the RV
was, then lowered it down off the flat-bed and winched
them together, so the day care center could become

a living room. Seeing her father so pleased as his new
get-away cabin took shape made Allie happy, too,

and though she felt a little weird back home when he
called her over to his computer screen to ask which
of the women on the Christian Personals site seemed
most like her mother, she eventually began to search
each face, choosing at last the one with the brown
eyes and sweet smile who could almost have been

her mother, and besides, said in her quote how much
she liked long walks in the woods, which was exactly
what Allie's mom liked, too. But when Winona
showed up in the new cabin that fall to meet Leroy,
she turned out to be older and fatter than in
her online photograph, and there was no way,

Allie told herself, her mother would wear a denim
top and jeans like that, or boots with skinny heels.
"This is my little girl," her dad said, but Allie
was already walking toward the door that led into
the living room add-on, where she reached up above
her own .410 shotgun on the wall and got down

her father's loaded 12-gauge, tears stinging
her eyes, for it was as if her mother had died all
over again. "You are not my mother," she declared
to Winona in her mind, starting up the trap machine
in the backyard, and it felt good as the gun, too big
for her, kicked back against her shoulder, and better

when she hit a clay pigeon and blew it to bits,
so that her father came running outside to stop her,

just as she had hoped. Yet this wasn't her old dad,
who would have been mad she took his shotgun
and told her so, but her new, talkative dad with sadness
in his eyes, who said Winona didn't like the noise,

though he himself didn't mind it, and anyway,
wouldn't she rather take his gun down to the secret
meadow and add Mr. Turkey to the rabbit and quail
she'd already checked off her list for the Four-Point
Crown contest, since afterward all she'd have left
was the deer? Allie turned toward the pine woods,

where he was pointing, mainly to hide the tears
starting up all over again, which only got worse
as she walked with the 12-gauge among the trees,
because how, she asked herself, could she even
think about the contest knowing he and Winona
were together back at the cabin? Then a small flock

of turkeys walked into the light of the secret meadow
ahead of her, right where her dad said they would be,
and suddenly she was all business, fitting the butt
of the gun into her shoulder, and aiming a little below
the head of the biggest one to accommodate the recoil.
"A natural," was what her father called her, grinning

with pride just like her old dad as Allie walked
into the yard with the large bird over her shoulder,
its wings fanning out behind her back. When Allie
laid it in the grass beside the gun, he went right
down on his knees to spread out its wings and didn't
even notice Winona staring at the bloody head

as if she were about to be sick, but Allie noticed.
Cleaning the bird in the sink after supper, all except
for the plumage, according to contest regulations,
she was almost afraid to touch the little head
with a closed eye on one side and a dangle of wattle
on the other. Then she put Winona's expression out

of her mind and thought only of her old, proud dad
on his knees in the grass opening up the enormous
wings in her own moment of pride, and that night,
as she lay in her RV bed listening to her father
talk on and on about trying to push the stone
off his heart, and Winona describe her two

daughters and her beautiful home up in Springfield,
Allie drew the pillow over her head and made
herself dream of her moment. Yet in the dream
she held the limp, warm quail again in her hand
after she shot it, and parted the dead fur of the rabbit
to find the red hole in its side, and when she walked

out of the woods toward her father with the turkey
over her shoulder, it was so heavy she could hardly
lay it down in front of him. In his shocked face
as he went down on his knees and wept she saw
she had brought the bodies of her mother and sister,
their eyes closed forever, and now he leaned

over them in the grass, spreading out their arms
and hands. Allie was relieved when she woke
to find her father right there on her bed, tugging on
her arm, and she was glad when he shook his head
and told her that Winona was gone, probably for good.
Only after she hugged him as hard as she could

did she begin, in spite of herself, to miss Winona.
For all she had now was the bloody, clotted
turkey feathers she found in the RV sink,
and the gun rack on the far wall where her mom
once kept kids' toys, and her dad checking out
the back window for a deer in the south field,

which, in this very instant, he happened to see. "Son
of a frigging bitch," he whispered, meaning how big
the doe was, then grabbed his Marlin off the wall
and fired it out the door before he even thought to give
Allie the kill for the Four-Point Crown. "Oh baby,
I'm sorry, I'm so sorry," he said on the way

to the deer he had dropped in the field, but walking
by his side in her pajamas, Allie was just sorry
for the deer, which had its eyes wide open
when they got there. "Shoot it! Shoot it!"
said her father, holding out his Marlin. "It's yours
on the second kill!" Yet neither she nor the deer,

which knew her heart, and did not expect to die,
could hear him. "Are you the one who has come
to save me?" asked the doe from down among
its helpless legs. And Allie, who had dreamed
of death, and only wanted to say yes, fell weeping
to her knees in the grass and could not stop saying no.

THE AMERICAN FLAG CAKE

Mae couldn't help feeling a little proud she wasn't
the one who got the stroke, being eighty-seven
and older than her brother Homer when he went down
in his driveway reaching for the door of the Cadillac
he loved, though at the same time she wanted to imagine
him just as he was the year before, so she arrived

at the annual Fourth of July Sykes family reunion,
already underway, with peach cobbler just as he'd
always asked for it, heavy on the peaches, setting it
on the food table next to the American flag cake.
Her granddaughter Debbie, at Mae's house in the Ozarks
for the weekend from Montana with her two kids,

could tell the stroke was bad from how her grandmother,
not a chatterer, chatted all the way over in the car
about Homer being the family's best cotton-picker when
he was only six, or making twenty-five cents apiece
from the skins of rabbits he caught in his home-made
traps. "He looks terrible," Mae's son Chip whispered,

and she had to admit he did, sitting in his wheelchair
beside his Arizona daughter, two tables over
from the other veteran, Shelby, who'd shown up
from Texas and wasn't doing so well himself.

He'd had his mouth wired shut, not from combat,
though he'd done tours in both Iraq and Afghanistan,

but from getting punched in the face by his new wife's
two grown sons. "You look great, Sir," said Leroy,
shaking Homer's hand, meaning Homer didn't.
"How you doing, young man," said Floyd, meaning
Homer wasn't. "Here's a little medicine for what ails you,
Mr. Sykes," Travis said, holding out his bottle of beer.

Looking up to their uncle all their lives for how tough
he was as a soldier and how rich he got afterward,
none of them really wanted to be staring down at that
lid folded over the left eye, nor wanted to feel
what it might be like for Homer to wear it, so they went
back to their table beside the two tubs of Bud Light,

where the other thirty and forty-something husbands
in baseball caps sat without their wives or second
wives and kids, making wisecracks at each other,
partly for Donna, Chip's second wife, who'd been cooking
with the other women for three days, and now sat
in a lawn chair near the tubs with her empties,

laughing at what she judged to be the wittiest remarks.
Everybody here knew the story of Donna's mother,
so gone to partying and alcohol her face turned a dark
gray color, and some were thinking Donna might
end that way herself, but in families there were things
you didn't say to a person, storing them up

from phone calls or visits one-on-one where you first
heard them, while confessing something in confidence
which got spread until everybody knew your story, too.

Sometimes, as was the case of Sissy and her mother, Mae,
what the Sykeses knew made them avoid each other,
but Sissy took a heaping plate of food straight

over to Homer's table and rubbed his back,
even though she'd known for years how her uncle
had left his wife and two daughters all on their own
while he advanced his military career. In fact Sissy
had adopted the son of Homer's younger daughter,
just twenty-nine when she got behind the wheel

of her car on drugs and killed herself. "I can serve
you however much you want," Sissy said, as if
the right quantity of sweet or scalloped potatoes,
or fried chicken or okra, or barbequed beef or pork,
or noodle casseroles, or the creamy fruit salad
she'd made with marshmallows in it, could bring back

the one thing everyone at the reunion wished for: Homer
the way he had been, the hero who gave the family
status with the medals he won in battle and his success
as a real estate broker in Saint Louis, and who had
that look of sorrow on his face even when he laughed,
so you could sense how hard it was for him

to put his feelings aside and get on with it. This,
for Sissy, was his true toughness. Old cheerleader,
who began with a child out of wedlock in high school
and now had two more by a husband who spent his spare
time gambling on credit cards in Branson, she had her
own history of sorrow, which Homer, without speaking

a word, always seemed to understand. But nobody here
could have wanted the old, tough Homer who never
spoke about his feelings back any more than Homer
himself. Since the stroke, though, he couldn't trust
his tongue to say what it was supposed to, and then he
couldn't clearly recall what it had said. Had he just

told Sissy to get free from her worthless husband
and live the one life she'd been given, or had he only
thought it? And when he turned to discover his daughter
Kim had drunk at least one Corona for each of her four
failed marriages, did he really say her problems were
all his fault? No matter, he could see from the way

they were studying his lips, trying to figure out what
he meant, that he'd been saved from himself, and now
the Sykeses were leaving their beers and half-empty
paper plates to gather for the annual photograph
around shrunken, bestroked Homer, who smiled on one
side of his face for the camera above a flag somebody

had taken from the cake and stuck in his shirt pocket.
Then, after everybody lined up for a helping of cake
and Mae served Homer his piece with a big square
of her peach cobbler, their little brother Wendell began
thumping the microphone. Standing beside Homer's
table with his dyed hair and comb-over, he seemed

unable to make up his mind whether he wanted to be
a venerable elder or a man who looked younger than
his age, and when he began tearing up about the old
back forty and how his mother had to sell her antiques
in the Depression, you would never have guessed
he was born in the good days, after she and their father

left the farm and started the laundry in Jeff City.
Never serving in the military didn't prevent Wendell
from choking up about the meaning of sacrifice
for freedom's call, either, or saluting the two veterans
in the house, Shelby, recovering from the violence
of his stepsons, and Homer, shaking his head no,

while Wendell signaled his son J.B., who had the same
comb-over and beefy look of authority as his father,
to start the applause. Don't you even think about
heckling him, Homer told the wrong part of himself,
but then Wendell, his chin trembling all over again,
asked his question: "What would Harlan Wesley Sykes,

the preacher, who started this clan in Mount Zion, say
if he could look out and see us all today?" And suddenly,
as the Sykeses wept and waved their tiny American flags
from the cake and cheered for themselves, the feeling
Homer had held back for a lifetime seemed to rush
into his chest, and he was rising from his wheelchair,

looking out over Sissy's rec room with his sad face
as if he were the old patriarch Wendell had called for,
trying to find words that might convey the pain that
grew inside him as he thought about these repugnant
strangers, who were the family and extended family
he'd always known, his brother, in love with war,

so long as he could stay home, Shelby, who'd brought
the war home with him, his nieces and beer-bellied
nephews with their appetites for food and beer
and credit-cards, and their blended and reblended
offspring, fighting over the remotes to play video games
on the two plasma TVs. Somebody, somewhere

was always doing the fighting, Homer thought,
including himself, the one who had spent the first
part of his life getting badges for it, and the rest
making money, while he ignored this deep
feeling which now he couldn't put aside, this bolt
of lightning electrifying his chest as he held it fast,

opening his mouth to express the wild pain of it,
his final testimony, that made Wendell's wife
Amy-Lou scream into her cell phone for an ambulance
and brought the whole Sykes family reunion to a stop.
Weird and scary, was how Debbie described what Homer
had uttered into the microphone, talking to her new

boyfriend that night on her cell as she toked up
in the gazebo to calm her nerves. But Sissy's husband,
Bob, said it sounded like a song he'd heard in Branson
about your luck running out, which made Sissy cry all
the more. At the hospital, where Homer lay near death,
Mae remembered a long, whispered chant that seemed

to have her own name in it. It took Amy-Lou,
the religious one, until breakfast the next day to figure
the whole thing out, how it wasn't really Homer at all
who sang or whispered or said whatever it was he said,
but the old preacher, Harlan Sykes, who'd come back
through Homer to speak to them in tongues, a sign,

she said, I'm dead serious, that we Sykeses might
be on some kind of special mission. Nobody believed it
at first, but the more Wendell cried and swore that he
was prompted the day before by some unseen force
to say the patriarch's name, and the more they thought
about Homer, the old soldier, standing up to sacrifice

himself for the family good, the more the Sykeses
bonded during the clean-up, drinking the leftover wine,
so as not to waste it, and tossing away the paper plates
and plastic cups and bowls and forks and knives and
spoons, and dumping the half-eaten casseroles and okra
and potatoes and meats, and throwing out the flag cake.

TEARS

From how matter-of-fact Mae was when she called,
starting out with the heat they'd been having
in Missouri, not so bad if you kept the fan on
and the back door open, and going on to her right
knee, about the same as it was before, Ruth could tell
something was eating at her, which turned out

to be the troubles their baby sister, Myrna,
had described on the phone from Texas
the night before, the very last thing Ruth
wanted to hear about, she said, because hadn't
Myrna ignored them all these years, thinking
she was better than anybody else, just like

when they were kids, and she and her twin
were Mama's favorites? "What goes around
comes around," Ruth added, adjusting her baseball
cap, back home for months from the acute care center
and surer of herself than ever. "That's the point,
Ruth," Mae said calmly. "It just come around." Now,

she had Ruth's attention, beginning to explain
how Myrna's rich, brilliant lawyer husband, Sherwood,
got Parkinson's so bad he was dropping folders
and documents right on the courtroom floor, and how

his mouth gradually went on a slant with a hole
where Myrna sometimes had to feed him,

and how – this was when Mae really began to feel
bad for her – he walked out of their bedroom
one day wearing her best dress, with pink lipstick
scrawled on his mouth, asking her with his hand
on his hip if she liked what she saw, of all the ways
to ask her. "The doctors claimed the whole thing

was caused by the overstimulation of his brain
from the implants they put in him to slow down
the shaking," Mae said, but the two sisters, recalling
together that Sherwood, never mind how brilliant
he was, seemed to speak and act a little funny
long ago when they first met him, weren't convinced.

"Lyle had his own problems in them days," Mae said,
remembering to herself how she waited night after night
for her husband outside the local bar in the truck
with two small, hungry kids. "But at least it wasn't
them problems." As for Ruth, who once waited at home
with three kids for the husband that never came back,

she almost thought she would prefer the cross-dressing,
and to her surprise, found herself saying so. "You know
you don't mean that," Mae answered, but when Ruth
went on to declare she did mean it, absolutely,
and Mae began to compare in her mind what it might
be like for Lyle to wear a dress rather than beat up

their kids, all pictured on the wall beside her recliner
as she frowned into the phone, she reckoned maybe

Ruth was right after all, changing the subject just
to get the thought of Lyle with his hand on his hip
out of her mind. "After that, Myrna told me, when
it got hard for Sherwood to speak at all, he started in

with his mirrors, having one installed in every
room of the house." Ruth thought for a minute
about the inconvenience of traveling on her walker
all the way to her bathroom mirror, the only one
she had, to primp a little each time the UPS man
she had a crush on swung into her driveway

with a new order of supplements. "That don't seem
so terribly weird to me," she said. "But you don't know
what kind of mirrors," Mae replied, "odd sizes,
for one thing, from small to full-length, all made up
special so when you looked into them, one nostril
or eye was too big, or your face and body was all

wavy, or divided up, as if you was looking through
the lines of your bifocals or trifocals." "Or fourfocals,"
Ruth added as she imagined finding her own face
all divided up like that in the bathroom mirror
while the UPS man waited at the door. "My God,"
Ruth said, feeling sick to her stomach. "I told Myrna,"

Mae continued, "that at my age I have all I can do
just to deal with a regular mirror, and the shock
that the person in it is actually me. Which was when
Myrna broke down right on the phone," Mae said,
"because Sherwood was trying to say the same thing
I told her – that I didn't know who I was anymore –

with his mirrors about himself as his Parkinson's got
worse, and to to top it off, wanted her to look into each
new one he made up so she could see what he meant."
Mae paused, recalling her nightmare about Myrna
in tears peering into mirror after mirror with her face all
mixed up each time in a different way. "Now don't

tell me this don't sound so terribly weird," Mae warned
her older sister, hoping a little, at the same time,
Ruth might do just that. But Ruth was noticing
the dark shadows her grow lights cast across the piles
of newspapers around her and the bags of clothes
falling out of the dark closet doorway in the hall,

thinking suddenly about how mixed up she herself
had somehow got, and how lonely and old
she was. "Is that all?" she asked herself out loud.
"Is that all there is?" And Mae said no, there was this
other mirror, the great big one Sherwood installed
on the stairway landing, which made you see yourself

as a tiny head, way up high, in the same moment
you had vertigo from the feeling of falling straight
down, so it was like you were watching yourself
lose yourself. "The first thing Myrna would see
coming downstairs toward the landing in the morning
was that poor man's shaky hand reaching out

so she would come and be there with him," Mae said,
which gave Ruth vertigo so strong she was suddenly
back in 1985, the start of her mixed-up, lonely life,
when she discovered her second husband, Paul,

reaching out his dead, yet living hand as if for hers
from down under the car that had rolled off its blocks

while he was trying to fix it and killed him. "Poor
Myrna Rose!" Ruth cried out, startling her sister,
"right when it was all going along so well for her."
This was the part of the phone call Mae made that night
she couldn't get over when she hung up, Ruth realizing
just how she herself had come to feel about Myrna Rose

and Sherwood, who weren't better than everybody else
after all, but had their own problems, which in the end
only family could appreciate. Mae lay down and slept
straight through without a single bad dream, but Ruth
didn't sleep at all, or thought she didn't, sleep being
for people who had nothing more constructive to do.

She stayed up to cut out magazine articles, saving
them in a pile by her chair as she worried about Myrna
breaking down, then closed her eyes, suddenly seeing
when she woke that she and Mae, getting so lathered up,
had forgot how Myrna always cried about her problems
as a kid, too spoiled to know life has no use for tears.

GRATITUDE

It was the December breakfast meeting at the Ava
Chamber of Commerce, and the blinking Christmas
lights over the crèche on one side of the podium
were red, white, and blue to go with the flag
on the other side, for the speaker was Elgin Sykes,
back from his final deployment to Afganistan,

the last of six tours for his nation, starting
way back with the Gulf War, as Billy Coons put it
in his introduction, which is, I got to tell you,
he smiled, enjoying the limelight as the Chamber's
President, unbelievable to me. Seated at the head
table with his mother, his little daughter Myla,

and Ava's oldest veteran, Paul Allen Dell,
Elgin would have recognized Billy's grin anywhere,
having seen it first as a boy in eighth grade, walking
in sorrow down the school hall inside the steel brace
with the bar between his legs that clicked
with each step. They were all here, the ones

who watched him as he graduated to crutches,
swinging his legs up as high as he could
before his feet came down to rest in his steel
shoes, and when his hip healed jig-jagged after

the operation in his freshman year, they saw him
begin all over again with the brace that clicked,

saying with their eyes as they parted in the school
lobby to let him pass how glad they were
that they weren't him. Yet today, as Elgin took
the podium with ribbons and medals on his chest, free
of his portable metal cage, and his former schoolmates
applauded him instead, he felt for a wonderful

moment as if he were entering the very dream
that had sustained him for years. Still, in the dream
they were all in high school, and now it struck him how
those years had actually happened to them, Billy,
leading the applause, a fat guy in real estate,
Hoyt, in the black suit, who inherited the family

funeral home, Clyde, the bald-headed banker,
who'd brought his wife Peggy, once a cheerleader
with breasts that weighed on Elgin's outcast heart,
now heavyset, covered with bling, and waiting
for him to speak. But Elgin, a different man himself
since he'd come back from his deprogramming in Texas,

was discovering, with a dismay that caught his tongue,
his mother had gotten old too, her hair showing streaks
of gray he somehow hadn't noticed. As she lifted
and held Myla on her lap to give her a better view,
he found himself recalling how, after his father left,
she lifted him into her arms to sit him down

on the toilet, and held him close to drag him up
the steps of the school bus while the driver just
sat and watched. Why had he not thanked her

each time, he asked himself, with a pain in his heart
he'd never felt before. So when he began
his speech at last, he didn't address the group,

anxious to hear the town hero, who'd returned
from serving the greatest nation on earth, describe
his triumph, as in his dream; he spoke with a strange,
urgent voice that surprised even him to his mother,
who'd begged him not to serve at all, telling her
how amazing she was. Who else in this whole room

was there to stand him up on the floor of the bus
and whisper into his ear, handing him his lunch,
that the driver was an ignorant asshole, Elgin said,
or to help him into the cargo space of the hatchback
after school, the only forward observer in Iraq
who got his training by watching the town of Ava

go backwards out the rear window. None of them,
staring at him as they held their coffee cups
or their forks over the last of their eggs, laughed
at the funny way he spoke about his service,
including Jimbo Starks and Charlie Webb, who rode
the school bus back then, and anyhow, with Elgin

talking only to his mother in that strange voice,
and her starting to cry, it didn't feel like a joke.
Had something gone wrong with Elgin's mind
when the military sent him to Texas last summer?
Jimbo asked Billy the next day, taking his lunch order
at Jimbo's Dog House while recalling that his wife

had seen Elgin's mother crying in August at Walmart.
But Billy declared it was all part of the homefront
syndrome, where your veteran, he said, gets it into
his mind that the people back home don't understand
the war and his sacrifice. It wears off after counseling,
he said, he'd seen a program about it on *Dr. Phil*

and it wasn't that big a deal. Yet this didn't explain
why Billy got so upset the morning before
about the language Elgin was using for the bus driver
right in front of the Chamber; or why the sacrifice
Elgin cared most about as he spoke, with tears
rimming his own eyes, belonged to his mother,

going straight on through Billy's abrupt call
for questions from the audience to thank her, first,
for telling him straightaway after his second divorce
from a cheating wife that his brains were all
in his pants, and then, for taking care of Myla
for most of the past year after he got thrown

by the blast of a Taliban IED. And when
the main doctor down in Texas released him
to come home, Elgin added, and he still couldn't
bear the high-pitched sound of his own daughter's
laughter, he should have thanked her for calling
the doctor up to thank him, at the top of her lungs,

for nothing. Was this the end of his speech?
Elgin, out of breath and looking around the room
at the astonished faces looking back at him,
couldn't say for sure himself, but as his mother
searched through her handbag for more Kleenex,
Paul Allen Dell, the old, deaf veteran at her side,

stood up to offer a loud applause, and Billy, seizing
his opportunity, went to the podium, threw his arm
around Elgin, and called him the man who helped
to make our way of life possible, which is, he said,
the envy of every nation on the globe. Now all of them,
the owners of the main drag of Ava, Missouri, rose

to applaud, some putting up their thumbs, some
going up to shake Elgin's hand before they shrugged
on their coats and headed out the door to open
their shops, agencies and companies, leaving behind
their dirty dishes and Paul Allen Dell, hunched
over his baby steps, to take up a distant rear.

So none of the others were there to see Elgin's mother,
uncomfortable with expressions of love, brush
an imaginary fleck of dust from the lapel
of his uniform and say how much she enjoyed
his speech as Elgin looked down at her, studying
her face and hair. Then he held her in his arms

and said thank you, this time for just growing old,
which had made her beautiful, he said, a word
he had almost forgot, causing her to weep all
over again in the blinking red, white, and blue light
of the crèche, while Myla, nudged between them,
cried to hear how loud her grammy cried.

HER SECRET

Why her husband must spread his things over every
table, counter-top, and chair, just like his mother Ruth,
Dolly no longer asks, knowing he will only answer as if
speaking to someone in his head who's keeping track
of all the ways she misunderstands him and wants

to hear over and over that he's sick and tired,
though that's just what he is, and how, anyway,
can she resent him for that? – so sick he has pill vials
for his bad circulation, bad heart, and nerve disorder
scattered around the kitchen sink, so tired

after staying up all night at his computer feeding
medication to the stinging in his legs, he crashes
for one whole day into the next. "Thurman?" she asks,
coming home from work to find him lying on their bed
in his underpants, still as the dead, his radio on

to tape the talk shows he's missing, and then the old
thought that he really is dead comes into her mind
all over again, so strong this time she can't
get rid of it, even after she sees him with her
own eyes just above the partition in the kitchen

making coffee in the way he's invented, boiling
the grounds, then putting in more grounds and a raw
egg, his bald head going back and forth under
the fluorescent light like the image of his continuous
obsession, which she can't escape and can never enter,

though now it's her own obsession that troubles her.
Stupid is her word for it, the same word he always
uses for the crazy things she gets into her head,
and it was stupid, still thinking Thurman was dead
though he was right there in front of her, and then,

when she tries to make herself stop, her heart starts
pounding until she can hardly breathe. "It is nothing
more than simple anger," the pastor tells Dolly
after the service at the church in Seymour
she attends each Sunday with the other women

who live nearby, and he recalls with a frown
of disappointment the anger he discovered in her heart
during their talk a year ago. How, she wonders,
could she have forgotten that after she wiped away
her tears in that earlier conversation about Thurman's

leaving things he wouldn't let her touch on every
surface in the house, even the couch and chairs,
the pastor made her see the malice she had carried
so deep inside not even she understood that all
this time she had been gradually filling the spare room

and the closed-in porch with her own discards,
broken figurines, old mops and mop pails and Christmas
decorations, out of a secret revenge. "And now,"

the pastor shakes his head, "this thought about your
husband, whom you have pledged to honor, lying

in his underpants, dead, the day before your fortieth
anniversary." When Dolly returns home at last
and opens the door to find the two pairs of sneakers
next to the recliner with the ankle brace in it,
and old videos on top of the half-read magazines

and newspapers by the TV, and the bathrobe and shirts
and pants folded over the backs of chairs, she does not
feel, as she sometimes has, that she might suffocate,
but instead, a relief that Thurman hasn't risen yet.
He won't mind, she thinks, that she's used one

of his sticky notes when he has read the words
she writes on it, I still love you, meaning how sorry
she is for blaming him behind his back to the pastor,
and for the secret anger she has kept so long
in her heart, yet because, unlike most things

in that house, it is hers alone, Dolly continues
to ponder the anger and keep it, even after Thurman
takes the note from the screen of his computer
with a smile, and gets his camera out to take
the anniversary photo he takes each year for his emails

of her holding plastic flowers, irritated with her
because she never could pose right, then sitting down
among the wires and the stacks of CDs and computer
paper to photoshop it, going over and over her teeth
and eyes to whiten them and taking all the wrinkles out

of her face until she looks like an old baby. "Oh,
this is nice," Dolly says when he brings the picture
to her, sitting on her small rocker in the only
uncluttered corner of the house, and she almost
means it, she has become so calm in her pondering

as she looks out the window and through the other
window of the closed-in porch, where a flock
of the migrating birds she loves linger for a time
under the roof of her feeder, and in an unaccountable
moment, lift their wings all together and fly away.

THE LOST CHILD

Remembering all the sorrow at the last Sykes reunion,
when the family patriarch and war hero, Homer,
went down at the microphone with his fatal stroke
speaking the words that didn't go together, partly
to the Sykeses and partly to the dark that gathered
around them, as it gathered now around the last beers
floating on ice water in the tub and the paper plates

strewn across the lawn, the holdouts in Sissy's gazebo
didn't want to hear Faylene sobbing full-out like that,
but Mae, the white-haired fixer of Sykes family conflicts,
was sure she could find a way to stop it. Yet Faylene
only shook her head no when Mae asked with a smile,
"Could it be back pain from the walking you done
today, Honey?" jiggling the red walker with wheels

and a hand brake that rested across Faylene's lap, and no
some more when Mae's son Daryl, who'd noticed how fat
Faylene had got since last year, wondered if it was a bad
combination of the wine and the heat, adding helpfully
that he'd been watching her sweat. Then Sissy,
Faylene's first cousin and confidante sitting beside her,
whispered into her ear, was this about her husband back

in Texas, who never took her anywhere, including here,
because he was too damn busy with his hubcap business,
and Faylene, reminded by all her Ozark relatives'
attention of the sadness in her life, sobbed even
louder, crying out at last, "My father Avery
was a turd." Nobody thought about Homer Sykes
at all after that, except his daughter, Kim.

She recalled in that moment how Homer never
came home from the military when she was a kid
needing a father, and decided he was a turd, too.
"You don't mean that, Honey," Mae said, still jiggling
the walker, but her brother Wendell, who had always
believed the guy who married their sister, Lana Bell,
was a high-toned son-of-a-bitch, hoped Faylene

did mean it. Wearing an uncle's expression of concern,
he went over and stroked her arm, saying she shouldn't
speak ill of her father now that both he and her mother
were dead. This was how he got her to tell him
what Avery did to Lana's photograph album,
cutting her dead first husband out of all the pictures
with scissors, and even cutting her head off

in one of them, where the husband had his arm
around her shoulder, and now that her parents
were gone, Faylene added, drying tears with the back
of her hand, and there was no more Avery to hide
her mother's car keys and accuse her of things
he imagined with other men, she couldn't stop thinking
of a little girl all alone, as she called herself, with no

brothers or sisters, sneaking out that album over
and over to find the same holes in it, which were like
the happiness Avery had stolen from both of them,
she said, all the while holding hands with her mother
like they were love-birds in front of his high-class
friends. "I could almost see why Wendell done it,"
Mae said afterward, trying to explain the whole thing

to her older sister Ruth on the phone. "Why Wendell
done what?" asked Ruth. "Why he got all red in the face
and started speaking ill of Avery himself – worse
than ill, really – calling him a blowhard who thought
he knew it all, but didn't know anything about the boy
nobody could of cut out of the album because
he wasn't even in it, the one that got Lana Bell

pregnant at fifteen, when Mama packed up
her things and sent her out East to live with you
and have the baby," Mae said. "Which I could almost see
why Wendell done," she repeated, fearing how angry
Ruth, who had the worst temper of all the Sykeses,
was going to be that their little brother had blurted
this old family secret sealed away for years.

"Not that he should of done it," Mae added. But Ruth
didn't seem to get mad, and when Mae went on to tell her
about how hard Faylene took what Wendell had said –
crying so, it would break your heart about her poor,
unknown brother or sister with no family, a lost child,
just like herself – there was no sound from the other end
of the phone except for the amazed, excited

voices on Ruth's TV and her radio, talking
at the same time about something for sale. "That
was when I decided to call you up, Ruth, and find out
what happened to that child," Mae said, relieved
to have got these words out at last. Now she felt a bit
teary herself, though having no tolerance for tears,
she let them build up in her nose so she could get

rid of them by blowing it hard one time. Meanwhile,
her actual sister, who was not the one Mae imagined
at all, stared confusedly out through her tilted
glasses at the pathways around her chair, one
trailing off through stacks of magazines toward
the kitchen, another heading past the grow lights
and sacks of fertilizer and piles of clothes to disappear

down the hall into the dark, wondering who,
exactly, this Faylene was, anyway. Oh, Ruth
remembered Wendell all right, the baby brother
that her mother had late, and spoiled rotten,
and she recalled her baby sister Lana Bell,
but now she was thinking about how her mother
had spoiled Lana and her twin Myrna, too,

giving them both movie star names, while Ruth,
the oldest of the seven kids, got the Bible name,
the switch, and all the house chores. "I am
the lost child, Mama," Ruth declared, then
tugged on her baseball cap, repeating herself
with more conviction, so there was no mistaking
what she had said. Soon, the whole Sykes family

was repeating it. Surprised and alarmed, Mae called up
Ruth's middle son, the one who understood his mother
had a good side, then phoned Amy-Lou, Wendell's wife,
who told Wendell, who called everybody he could
think of, more mournful each time that the sister
he never liked seemed to be losing her grip again,
and more pleased with his importance as the person

bearing the news. "Tell Aunt Ruth we're rooting
for her," Faylene wrote to Amy-Lou on Facebook,
thanking her for the photos of the reunion, especially
drawn to the one where she was smiling in the gazebo
beside Sissy and you could hardly see her walker. "Can't
wait till next year," she said. She never mentioned
the lost child, and as the Sykeses all emailed

their reunion photos to each other and searched
for the ones that showed them smiling, too,
even the holdouts who had listened to Faylene cry
in the gathering darkness wanted to be back there
once more, where they were having so much fun.
Being lost wasn't an issue to Ruth now, either,
unless you counted her struggle over the phone

to identify Mae, who called to offer comfort on Ruth's
first night in the nursing home. "I'm the sister
with the husband that died the same year yours did,"
Mae explained, then listened to the distant voices
of commercials on the TV, while Ruth thought about
husbands and sisters and women getting cleaner counters
and kitchen floors. "The only one that's still alive,"

Mae added, then wished she hadn't, because
it made her think of how useless and dead she felt
in that moment as the family helper Faylene suddenly
didn't need and Ruth didn't even know. She wanted
Ruth to get mad at her about something, anything,
or maybe to explain how she could have said
she was a lost child, when they both knew

she was the strong and independent one. "Remember
how I always went to you for the answers when
we was kids?" she asked, and finding no answer, Mae,
who never cried, felt tears in her eyes. "Remember?"
she said again to the voices on the TV and the other
old woman holding the phone, Mae's tears coming
so fast now she didn't even think to blow her nose.

GOING HOME

Ruth couldn't believe she was riding down the road
on an outing instead of sitting in the afternoon circle
back at Elmwood, the home where her son had stuck her,
listening to young guy who didn't mean it clap and say
how wonderful it was when somebody tried to toss
a basketball through the low hoop at the center

of the circle and failed completely. Being up front
in the van with Ralph was like being invited to sit
in the front row of the one-room school in the Ozarks
after she got an A in spelling, or like riding to town
as her husband Paul drove the pickup with the kids
in the back, all on their way to sell vegetables and help

start up the nursery she missed so much. Now,
there weren't any kids in the back, only a bunch of old
women from Elmwood, who probably wanted to be
right next to Ralph like she was. But never mind them,
Ralph didn't care for old. Ruth could tell because
he chose her to ride with him, calling her "young woman"

as he lifted her up into the van and sat her down
so his face almost touched her face. This was when
he announced to the others that after they'd stopped
at McDonald's for snacks, he planned to drive by

Ruth's nursery, which she had told them so much about.
Even Ruth was surprised, since after she'd asked him

to take her there the last time, he'd told her
he couldn't find it. All he could see when he typed in
the address on Google Earth was trees, he said,
but Ruth didn't know what typing had to do with it;
to get there, you had to drive. Sometimes Ralph
could be even more obstinate than Paul was,

but she loved Ralph anyway, since unlike Paul, he
understood the need to pay attention to what
she said, like when she told him about the itch
she felt in her fingers that spring, longing to pot up
the forsythias and roses, or complained about
how dark they always kept it at Elmwood. "It's only

because you can't see," the nurses always told her,
but Ralph said that yes, sometimes it did get a little
dark before the staff turned the lights on at night.
Finally Ruth discovered the problem with her sight
was caused by the wrong prescription on her glasses.
She moved them up and down on her nose, looking

through them, then looking over them. "See?"
she asked Ralph, visiting in her room. "There's no
difference. These damn glasses don't change a thing."
It was dark outside the van window, too, yet
from the way the others behind her came to life
and started giving Ralph their orders for snacks,

Ruth knew they had arrived in the take-out lane,
and she could just make out the poster with burgers

coming toward them. She might have guessed Gloria
would order an ice-cream cone. Until Ruth had heard
Ralph chatting with Gloria yesterday at the next table
in the dining hall, she hadn't noticed how fat

Gloria was, and now, she understood why. Ruth
declined to order at all, and when Ralph offered
to share his fries with her as he started out
for the nursery, she said she couldn't possibly
find room for them, loud enough for Gloria to hear.
Soon, Ruth began to wonder if they had got off onto

the wrong road, thinking, it was so bumpy and dark,
she might be on her way from Missouri to north Texas
as a girl with her family in the truck on the way
to pick cotton, chairs tied to the roof and a dust
storm swirling around them. But just like her father,
Ralph was sure. "Don't worry. I have my GPS," he said.

Ruth was comforted because of how he said GPS
and also that he knew what it meant. Then
he was in the driveway of her home and nursery,
she knew from the crunch of gravel that slowly
came to a stop. "I'd know that sound anywhere,"
she told Ralph twice, so why did he keep asking her if

this was the right place? "Now I get why Google Earth
showed it as trees," Ralph said, looking at the enormous
tangle of overgrown shrubs and maples and bending
birches, all broken out of their pots. "It *is* all trees."
Behind the collapsing fence, the door of the sale shed
hung off one hinge. Ralph pulled up to the old house

with the algae on its shingles and buckling front steps.
"Is this the end of the line?" somebody asked from
the back. "I'm not getting out here," Gloria answered,
"no way." Her seat mate, waking up from a nap,
said, "Who would live in a dump like this? I thought
we were going to a place with flowers." Squinting

through her glasses, Ruth couldn't see her flowers
or much of anything else except a large sign outside
the van window. "For Sale," she read on the sign.
"This is a mistake," she declared. "My property's not
for sale." She was so upset about the sign on the way
back to Elmwood, she thought she was going to cry

until she realized at last that house wasn't hers at all,
Ralph had driven her to the wrong place. "You and your
GPS," she said, crossing her arms, refusing to speak
to him or the others who said those untrue, insulting
things about her home, determined now to make her son
get her out of Elmwood, and really take her home.

III · Why I Carried My Mother's Ashes

DANCING IN TENNESSEE

How was he to know, when his father left them
and his mother took him by the hand
to her clothes closet, screaming

because he did not understand how to behave
and because, alone and lost, she herself
did not understand how to behave,
that this was the room she led him to,

20B in the nursing home, where he sat
once more in the dim light among her slippers
and shoes, calling out to her, "Mama, Mama,"

though now she was right there
in her bed, half-deaf, eyes wide open
in her blindness, her teeth out,
breathing rapidly through her mouth?

How could he have known when she whipped him
as if she would never stop because his father
loved someone else, it was the shock

of this final unbelievable lovelessness
she was preparing him for? All gone, her years

afterward with the new man, and the house
and farm she helped build to replace

the hopes that she once had. Gone
to ruin, the house and the farm,
but never mind. And never mind

her lifelong anger, and all her failures
of the heart: this was not his mother.
Lying on her stroke side, her nose
a bony thing between her eyes that blinked

and blinked so he could see behind them
to her fear, she was a creature
whose body had failed, and he had no way

to reach except through her favorite song
he sang as a boy to lift the grief from her face,
and began to sing now, "The Tennessee Waltz,"
understanding at last that its tale of love stolen

and denied was the pure inescapable
story of her life – his father the stolen
sweetheart she never forgave

or forgot. It didn't matter that she could not
see him beside her there or, struggling for air,
she was unable to eat or drink
or sing. He took her good hand in his

and rocked her and sang for them both,
his mother discovering once more in the tips
of her fingers what touch was like,

and he discovering too, while he sang on
and on, stealing her back from this moment
in the small, dim room where she lay dying,
and they danced and danced.

WHY I CARRIED
MY MOTHER'S ASHES

Because her mother told her in the Ozarks
don't come running back.
Because it was too far to run back.

Because when my father left her
in the projects of Springfield, Vermont,

up all night sewing with three
kids upstairs, she went back anyway
in her mind. Because I looked up at her

bent over the Singer's tiny light
that hurt my eyes and left a scar

on everything I saw, the scar of her
rejection and hurt. Because I missed her
while she was right there beside me

disappearing into her work, then and in all
the years afterward, making a life

with my stepfather out of exhaustion
and self-denial and unrequited
longing. Because late on lonely nights

she phoned to hear the voices of her sisters
and brothers talking about nothing

at all, which was for her the dearest talk.
Because the wings of the plane
lifted me high above the rain clouds

of New England as I carried the ashes back
to the rolling fields and farmhouses and hot sun

of the country where she was born.
Because in the cooling twilight my old
widowed Aunt Dot waited for me

among family photographs in her small
apartment, and I lay down on the pump-up bed

by the fan on the floor. Because, when I woke,
I discovered her just as she had always been,
never mind the bad circulation

in her legs, up early bringing back her dead
husband and sister and brother in stories

where they lived with her children
and grandchildren while the toast popped up
and the ham and eggs fried.

Because as we arrived at the graves
of my grandmother and grandfather, my uncles

and their wives waited, too, Truman on a cane
smiling beside his Cadillac with his sorrowful face
and offering me his good hand,

and her baby brother, Wallace, the one
she never liked, shaking my hand and tearing up

while he called her a damn Yankee. Because
when they listened to me read Walt Whitman,
whom they did not know, asking them to look for him

under their bootsoles, all my uncles and aunts
bowed their heads and looked respectfully down

at their shoes. Because when Truman, the old soldier,
walked solemnly to the graves to spread
the ashes, he lurched to one side on his cane

with each step, bringing his shoulders up
erect and military. Because we held the small box

for each other, Dot for Truman, I for Wallace,
who tipped his bald head so I saw up close
the wide adhesive bandage from the operation.

Because as they reached inside, taking the gray
dust into their old hands, they must have felt

it was their dust, too, each of them speaking
to my mother in a soft, casual way as if
she stood there beside them in the cloud

that rose from the grass. Because they loved her,
as I did in this moment when she seemed

to join us, and I no longer missed her.
Because the voice I heard then was my own voice
saying a loud Amen, now mixed

with their Amens, all of us bound together
in this homeplace where I had carried my mother,

who would never need to run back to it,
or dream of it holding their voices to her ear,
because she would never, ever again, be gone.

ADDENDUM TO PART II:

SIX MAIN SYKES SIBLINGS
AND THEIR FAMILY CONNECTIONS

Ruth: Oldest of the six siblings in the Sykes family, which include Mae, Homer, Myrna Rose, Lana Bell and Wendell. Offspring are Thurman, an unnamed "middle son" and a third son not mentioned.

Mae: Second born of the siblings, married to Lyle. Offspring are Sissy, Chip, Daryl and Jo-Lynn.

Homer: Third of the siblings. Offspring are Kim and a deceased younger daughter, unnamed.

Myrna Rose: Fourth born, with her twin, Lana Bell. Married to Sherwood.

Lana Bell: Myrna's twin, married to Avery. Offspring are Faylene and the lost child.

Wendell: Last born, married to Amy-Lou. Son is J.B.

OTHERS

Leroy: Son of Homer's deceased daughter. Adopted and raised by Sissy. Offspring, Allie.

Elgin: Chip's son by his first wife, the unnamed mother of "Gratitude." Offspring, Myla.

ABOUT THE AUTHOR

Called by poet Philip Levine "one of the great storytellers of contemporary poetry," Wesley McNair is the author of twenty books, including *Lovers of the Lost: New and Selected Poems*, and *The Words I Chose: A Memoir of Family and Poetry*. He has twice been invited by the Library of Congress to read his poetry and has received prizes from *Poetry* and *Poetry Northwest* magazines, the Sarah Josepha Hale Medal, Guggenheim and Rockefeller Fellowships, and two grants in poetry from the National Endowment for the Arts. In 2006 he was selected for a United States Artist Fellowship. He is the Poet Laureate of Maine.

A NOTE ON THE TYPE

The Lost Child has been set in Jeremy Tankard's Kingfisher. The product of the designer's desire to create a readable, appealing text face that captured the vitality and color of historical models, Kingfisher draws on the features of a handful of classic book types without being an explicit revival or reinterpretation of any one type. Among the many noteworthy features, perhaps the most appealing is an intentional irregularity in the letterforms, a trait intended to capture the liveliness of types cut by hand. Inspired by Stanley Morison's 1926 essay, "Towards an Ideal Italic," Tankard developed the Kingfisher italic along the lines of the "sloped romans" of the early twentieth century, following the models established by Eric Gill in his Perpetua and Joanna italics to create a face that is a carefully harmonized counterpart to the roman.

DESIGN & COMPOSITION BY CARL W. SCARBROUGH